AF483081

Our Life Together – A Chronicle of Two Souls Intertwined

Our Life Together – A Chronicle of Two Souls Intertwined

Michael & Carolyn Byrd

Contents

Contents

The Life Chronicles of

Mr. & Mrs. ____

Married on ____

copyright

First Edition: October 20, 2023
ISBN: 979-8-218-30953-4

Printed in USA

Disclaimer: This journal is provided for informational purposes and personal use only. The authors and publisher are not engaged in rendering medical, legal, or professional advice. Any opinions expressed within this journal are solely those of the individual authors and do not necessarily represent the views of the publisher. It is recommended that you consult with professionals in the relevant fields to address specific concerns or issues.

Please visit our website at www.mikeandcarolbyrd.com for additional resources and information related to this journal.

Dedication

In Gratitude to the Couples Whose Journeys Have Inspired Us

Over the past 22 years, we have had the privilege of witnessing the incredible transformations of hundreds of couples. We have seen love blossom in the most unexpected places, mending what was once broken, and watched as you emerged from the storms of life stronger and more resilient than ever.

This journal is dedicated to each and every one of you, who, through your shared experiences, have illuminated the path for countless others. You have shown us the enduring power of love, commitment, and the beauty of creating visions within a relationship.

To those who have entrusted us with your stories, shared your triumphs and tribulations, and allowed us to be a part of your remarkable journeys, we extend our deepest gratitude. Your courage, vulnerability, and unwavering commitment to one another have been our greatest inspiration.

A special thanks goes to Shaq & Beril, who ignited a spark within us to revisit and enhance our original marriage journal. Your dedication to one another, your commitment to personal growth, and your shared vision for a deeper, more fulfilling life together have reminded us of the boundless possibilities that exist within a loving partnership.

As you embark on your own journey through these pages, may you find inspiration, guidance, and the tools you need to create a vision that transcends the seasons of life. Remember, it is in the shared vision, the unwavering support, and the deep, abiding love that you will discover the true essence of a lifelong partnership.

With heartfelt gratitude and warmest wishes,
Mike and Carol Byrd

Introduction

Every year, innumerable couples embark on the sacred journey of marriage, only to find themselves adrift in the sea of divorce. Often, the unraveling of relationships can be traced back to a dearth of understanding, shattered commitments, and a lack of heartfelt communication. When shared visions are absent, it becomes all too easy for two souls to drift apart, hindered by conflicting ideals that fail to align. In the realm of relationships, harmony must be carefully cultivated through the confluence of both partners' interests and aspirations. While unified as one, everyone brings forth a tapestry of life experiences that shape their unique essence. As personal trajectories unfold, so too must the journey that is shared as a couple evolve. By amalgamating dreams, values, and goals, a formidable unity and unbreakable bond can be forged. Dedicate precious moments to explore the facets that hold profound significance for both of you—a gift beyond price, which in turns creates a tapestry of indelible memories, while simultaneously laying the foundation for an uncharted future woven together.

Every relationship is a journey, a beautiful dance of love, understanding, and growth. As we move forward in this journey, let's remember that our bond is not just about the destination, but also about the joy of the journey. It's about the shared laughter, the comfort in silence, the strength in vulnerability, and the love that encompasses it all. As you fill this journal, remember, it's not just about the answers you write, it's about the conversations they spark, the understanding they foster, and the love they deepen. So, let's continue this journey of discovery, growth, and love.

This journal is unlike any other. It is a journal that unfolds in phases. Phase one is a sacred space where both individuals come together, sharing their deepest values, aspirations, and the concrete steps they will take to achieve their goals. Phase two is a journey, navigating through these stages of life side by side, supporting one another through thick and thin. Phase three emerges when they have traversed these chapters of life, gifting them the wisdom to reflect upon and journal about their insights and experiences. "Our Life Together" blossoms into a magnificent fabric of love, a cherished keepsake that holds the essence of their shared history, passed down as a precious heirloom for generations to come.

Chapter One – Our New Life Together as a Couple

Becoming One, Creating a Life of Togetherness

Welcome to the inaugural chapter of *"Our Life Together"*. This enchanting segment delves into the genesis of your symbiotic union, an exquisitely transformative process that gives birth to a world steeped in unity and harmony. The decision to forge an unbreakable bond with another soul is one that resonates deeply, surpassing mere emotions, and delving into realms of unwavering dedication, profound comprehension, and joint evolution. It entails crafting a life that embodies both your unique identities, shared aspirations, and individual aspirations.

In the genesis, there exists an enigmatic kindling, a magnetic force that unites two souls. This chapter delves into that initial bond, the intoxication of the blooming courtship, and the exquisite ambiguity that accompanies the dawn of a newfound partnership.

Landmark Moments

- **The First Date**: It had the potential to be both awkward and magical, yet undeniably, it marked the beginning of something truly extraordinary. Take a moment to ponder this very instant and allow the emotions it evoked to resurface within you. What comes to your mind?

- --
- **The First "I Love You"**: Saying these three profound words, for the very first time, marks a significant milestone in the journey of love. It represents a sacred promise filled with the depths of devotion and unwavering commitment shared by two souls entwined. An eternal question remains, hidden within the tender embrace of affection: Who, in this divine dance of hearts, had the courage to utter these three words first?

- --
- **Moving in Together**: This is the moment when you start to uncover the intricacies of cohabiting, whether it's through shared responsibilities or shared moments of happiness. Did you find this transition challenging?

- --

- **The Proposal**: A leap of faith, a promise of a shared future, and a moment of pure happiness. The proposal is like taking a bold step towards a lifetime together. Where and how did it take place?

  ____

  ____.

- **The Wedding Day**: The moment you both exchanged your vows, promising to be there for each other in every step of the journey called life. It's the milestone that signifies the beginning of your shared adventure. Can you recall the date when your hearts united in matrimony and the place where this beautiful celebration took place?

  ____

  ____

Reflect and Connect

Now is the time for both you and your partner to reflect and connect. Let's dive into some thought-provoking prompts to guide your discussion:

1. **Our Story**: Write down the story of how you both met. What attracted you to each other? What were your first impressions?

   Spouse #1

     Spouse #2 ____

   ----

2. **Shared Values**: Discuss and jot down the values that you both share. How do these values influence your relationship? ____

   ----

3. **Our Dreams:** What are your shared dreams and aspirations as a couple? Where do you see yourselves in the next 5 years?____________________________________

   ----

4. **Steps Towards Togetherness**: What steps can you take to strengthen your bond and enhance your togetherness?

   ----

5. **The Promise**: What does the commitment of marriage mean to you? What promises had you made to each other? ____

Remember, this journal is a safe space for you both to express your thoughts, dreams, and fears. It's not about right and wrong answers; it's about understanding, empathy, and growing together.

> *Becoming a couple can be compared to the fusion of two sparks, which then grow into one blazing flame, resulting in a magnificent and harmonious dance of togetherness that brings inspiration.*
>
> *– Mike & Carol Byrd*

Chapter Two – Purchasing Our First Home Together

Building Your Nest Together

This chapter delves into the enchanting milestone of acquiring your first home together. It revolves around crafting a dwelling that surpasses the mere notion of a house, and instead embodies a sanctuary that echoes your affection, aspirations, and the extraordinary journey you share.

- Values: Outline your shared financial values and homeownership goals.

  ____

  ____

- Goals: Determine your budget and what kind of home you want.

  ____

  ____

- Steps: Research, save, and plans to buy your dream home.

  ____

  - ____

  - ____

Landmark Moments

1. **The House Hunt**: Finding the perfect home can be an exhilarating journey filled with moments of exhaustion and immense joy. It's all about discovering a place that deeply resonates with your shared vision. What sparked your interest in the pursuit of finding a place to call home?

----

2. **The First Home Tour**: Walking into a potential home for the first time is a truly unforgettable experience. It's a moment filled with excitement and anticipation as you start picturing your life unfolding in this brand-new space. When you first laid eyes on that house, what did you envision?

----

3. **The Purchase**: The moment you sign the papers, and the house becomes your home. It's a moment of pure delight, accomplishment, and eager anticipation. The papers are signed, the deed is yours, and the smiles on both your face is beaming. You stride up to the entrance, holding the new keys to your future in your hand. The weight of the cool metal, promising a new chapter ahead, feels substantial in your palm. You insert it into the lock, turn it with confidence, and the door swings open. Share the experience when you received the keys?

----

4. Moving In: The initial step in transforming a house into a cozy home involves the exhilarating process of unboxing and organizing your belongings. How did you tackle the exciting task of moving in? Did you enlist the help of professional movers or just the two of you?

----

5. Making Memories: The excitement and joy of creating those unforgettable first memories in your new home is truly unparalleled – from the heartwarming moments of your first dinner together, to the excitement of welcoming your first guest, and even the occasional disagreement that only reinforces the love and life within your home. And now, what was that very first memory you made together in your cherished new abode?

Reflect and Connect

Here are some prompts that can help you reflect on your journey of creating your home:

1. Our Home: Write about your first home together. What did you love about it? What were some challenges you faced? ____

____

____

2. Shared Vision: Discuss your shared vision for your home. How did you envision its appearance and atmosphere? Were your visions aligned? ____

____

3. Making It Ours: What did you do to transform your house into a place that truly feels like home? ____

____

4. Our Memories: Share your favorite memory in your first home. How does recalling this memory make you feel? ____
____
____

A home is not simply four walls; it is a haven of love, solace, and unity. As you embark on this new chapter, treasure the memories and the journey that has brought you to create this extraordinary haven.

> Home is where love finds its rest.
> – Mike & Carol Byrd

Chapter Three – Preparation for Parenthood

Becoming Loving and Capable Parents

In this chapter, we delve into one of life's most profound journeys - parenthood. It's about transforming from a couple into a family, about nurturing a life, and about the immense love that fills your hearts.

- Values: List the core values you want to instill in your children.

- Goals: What kind of parents do you aspire to be? Set achievable parenting goals.

- Steps: Plan steps to prepare for parenthood, from childbirth classes to creating a safe environment. --

  ----

Landmark Moments

1. **The Decision:** The moment both of you made the life-changing decision to embark on the incredible journey of parenthood, what emotions were running through your hearts and minds?
Spouse #1 ____
Spouse #2 ____
2. **The First Positive Test**: Seeing that positive result on the pregnancy test, a wave of pure joy, excitement, and a hint of nervousness rushes through you. How did you choose to celebrate and share that incredible moment with your spouse?
____
____
3. **The First Kick:** Feeling the baby's first movement is truly a magical and awe-inspiring moment, which adds an extra touch of reality to this incredible journey of motherhood. Can you recall the precise moment when you first experienced the miraculous sensation of life stirring inside you?
____
____
4. **The Birth:** The moment you first saw your little miracle, it was a whirlwind of emotions, an overwhelming wave of exhaustion, and an indescribable love for this tiny human being. Can you put into words the overwhelming joy that surged through you when you laid eyes on your bundle of joy?   Spouse #1 ____
Spouse #2 ____

5. **The First Year:** Navigating through the sleepless nights, witnessing the first heart-melting smiles, cherishing the precious first words, and celebrating the magical first steps. This incredible journey of growth spans not only for the little one but also for you as proud parents. What are some of the unforgettable highs and the challenging lows experienced during that extraordinary first year.

Reflect and Connect

Here are some prompts to help you reflect on your journey towards parenthood:

1. Our Decision: Discuss the moment you decided to become parents. What were your thoughts   and feelings?

____

____

2. Our Hopes: What are your hopes and dreams for your child? ______________________

____

____

3. Our Fears: Parenthood can feel like a rollercoaster ride filled with both excitement and challenges. Share your fears, concerns and discover collaborative ways to conquer them together.

____

____ __________________

4. Our Growth: How has parenthood changed you individually and as a couple?

Spouse #1 ____

Spouse #2 ____

Remember, parenthood is not about being perfect; it's about being present. It's about love, understanding, and patience. It's about growing together as a family, one day at a time.

> "Parenting is a journey of love and self-discovery."
> – Mike & Carol Byrd

Chapter Four – Navigating Major Decisions

Making Informed Choices Together

This chapter delves into the vital aspect of every relationship - decision making. As a couple, you will encounter a multitude of decisions, whether big or small, that have a profound impact on your lives. The essence of this chapter lies in the art of making these decisions collectively, infused with love and respect.

- Values: List your shared values in decision-making.

  ____
- ____
- ____
- Goals: Set goals for making major life decisions collaboratively.

  ____

  ____
- Steps: Develop a decision-making process and communication strategy

  ____

  ____
- ____

Landmark Moments

1. **The First Major Decision**: The first instance you and your partner made a significant decision together; it could have entailed relocating to a new city, transitioning careers, or even adopting a furry friend. Can you recall the nature of the decision and elaborate on how it was effectively managed and resolved?

----

2. **The Disagreements:** Times when you found yourselves at odds on a matter of great importance. It's an integral part of any relationship, and it's crucial to navigate these moments with mutual respect and understanding. How did you successfully navigate through these challenges? ________________________

----

3. **The Compromise:** The moments of compromise, where one person prioritized the other's choice, hold immense significance in shaping relationships. These instances have the power to inspire and truly engage individuals on a deep level. How did these specific junctures impact the dynamics of your relationship?

----

4. **The Joint Decisions:** Decisions that you've made together, where both of you had an equal say and were happy with the outcome. What was the venture and how did you manage through it?

____

____

5. **The Impact:** Reflecting on how these decisions have influenced your life and fostered growth in your relationship. How have these choices molded and shaped the trajectory of your bond? ____

____

____

Reflect and Connect

Here are some prompts to help you reflect on your journey of decision making:

1. **Our Decisions:** One of the crucial aspects of any relationship is the decision-making process. It becomes even more important when it comes to major decisions that need to be made jointly. In your relationship, it is essential to discuss and navigate these decisions together. By doing so, you can ensure that both partners are involved and have a say in shaping your shared future.

----

2. **Our Process:** What is your process of decision-making as a couple?

----

3. **Our Learnings:** What have you learned from your disagreements and how have you grown.

----

4. **Our Future:** What is one major decision you foresee in your future? ____ How do you plan to approach it? ____ ____

Remember, decision-making is a process that requires open communication, understanding, and sometimes, a little compromise. It's these decisions that shape your journey and bring you closer as a couple.

> "Decisions made together carry the strength of unity."
> – Mike & Carol Byrd

Chapter Five – Building Financial Wealth

Financial Freedom and Security

This chapter encompasses a crucial aspect of your shared journey - financial planning. It revolves around constructing a foundation for a secure future, attaining financial independence, and making well-informed choices about your wealth.

- Values: Define your financial values and principles.

- --
- Goals: Set financial goals and milestones.

- --
- Steps: Create a financial master plan, including saving, investing, and debt management.

- --
- --
- --

Landmark Moments

1.**The First Joint Account:** The moment when you made the decision to combine your finances represented a significant milestone in your relationship, symbolizing a deepened sense of trust and shared responsibility. Could you describe this pivotal moment in your journey you shared as a
couple? ____
____
Additionally, were there any concerns or fears that arose during this process? ____

2. **The Savings Plan:** The development of your initial savings plan, a crucial step towards securing your financial future. How effectively are you navigating this plan? ____
____

3. **The Investments:** When embarking on your first joint investment, be it in a property, a business, or the stock market, what was the initial investment you made together?
____
____

4. The Milestones: When it comes to achieving your financial goals, such as paying off a mortgage, reaching a savings goal, or retiring a debt, which goal have you successfully accomplished? ____

5. The Financial Freedom: The day you realize that you have achieved financial stability and freedom is a momentous occasion in your shared journey. Can you recall the specific day, and can you vividly describe the events and emotions surrounding it?

____

____

____

Reflect and Connect

Here are some prompts to help you reflect on your financial journey:

1. Our Plan: Discuss your financial plan. What are your long-term and short-term financial goals? ____
2. Our Achievements: Reflect on your financial achievements. How did those achievements impact your life as an individual and in your relationship?
____

3. Our Challenges: What financial challenges have you faced and how did you overcome them?
____
____

4. Our Future: How do you plan to achieve financial security and freedom in the future?
____

Remember, financial planning is not just about money; it's about ensuring a secure and comfortable future for you both. It's about making decisions today that will ensure peace of mind tomorrow. We hope this chapter helps you navigate your financial journey.

"Wealth is not about the size of your bank account,
but the richness of your life."
– Mike & Carol Byrd

Chapter Six – Enriching Relationships

Deepening Friendships and Connections

In this chapter, we delve into the significance of nurturing connections beyond your romantic relationship. It's about fostering meaningful friendships, upholding connections, and enhancing your social life as a couple.

- Values: Identify values that nurture your friendships.

  ____
  ____

- Goals: Set goals for you both to maintain friendships.

  ____
  ____

- Steps: What steps can you both take to prioritize quality time with friends and personal development.

  ____
  ____
- ____
- ____

Landmark Moments

1. Our First Friends as a Couple: Meeting new friends together as a couple or introducing your partner to your circle of friends marks a significant milestone in your shared social life. Do you remember the first couple you and your partner befriended?
____

2. The Double Dates: Going on double dates, immersing yourselves in various relationship dynamics, and extracting valuable lessons from these experiences. How have these encounters enriched our journey as a couple?
____
____

3. The Support System: Leaning on your friends during challenging times and reciprocating the support when they need it. Have the two of you established a shared support system that positively impacts both of your lives? _______________________________
____

4. The Celebrations: Celebrating the important milestones in life alongside friends, creating cherished memories, and strengthening the bonds of friendship are all essential elements in the journey of life. Take a moment to reflect upon the significant milestones you and your friends have experienced together, and the precious memories that have been formed as a result. These shared moments of friendship serve as a constant source of inspiration, overflowing with engaging and heartwarming tales that bring joy and meaning to our lives.

----

5. The Balance: When it comes to balancing your life, it can sometimes feel overwhelming. However, it is crucial to cultivate a well-rounded life, as it is all about finding balance. Finding the right balance between your personal life, work life, and social life may be challenging and can induce stress, but it will ultimately lead to a more fulfilling and satisfying life. How have you managed to create a harmonious and balanced life together? _______________________

Reflect and Connect

Here are some prompts to help you reflect on your social journey:

1. Our Friends: Who are the friends you've made as a couple? How have they enriched your lives? ____

____

2. Our Support: Share a time when your friends were your support system. How did it strengthen your bond with them?

____
____

3. Our Balance: How do you balance your social life and personal life as a couple?

____
____

4. Our Future: What steps can you take to nurture and deepen your friendships and social connections? ____

____

Remember, enriching your social life is about more than just having fun. It's about building a community, learning from others, and offering support when needed. It's about growing as individuals and as a couple.

> "Friendships and connections are the tapestry of life."
> – Mike & Carol Byrd

Chapter Seven – Advancing in Life and Career

Navigating Career Choices Together

This chapter delves into the realm of your professional endeavors, with a primary focus on fostering mutual support for each other's career aspirations, commemorating notable achievements, and expertly navigating the various challenges that lie in wait.

- Values: List your career and personal development values.

- --
- --
- Goals: Set career advancement goals and priorities.

- --
- --
- Steps: Support each other's career aspirations and plan for growth.

- --
- --
- --

Landmark Moments

1. **The Career Goals**: Discussing your career goals and aspirations with each other is a critical step in fostering understanding and providing support. What are your aspirations for your professional journey?

Spouse#1____

Spouse #2 ____

2. **The Achievements:** Celebrating one another's triumphs, be they significant or trivial, cultivates an atmosphere of optimism and mutual esteem. By dedicating moments to recognize achievements, you pave the path for deeper bonds and connections within your relationship. How have you celebrated one another's achievements?

____

____

3. **The Challenges:** Supporting one another during difficult periods, such as transitions in employment, promotions, or even the loss of a job, is a pivotal aspect of a strong and resilient partnership. Reflecting on our journey together, what remarkable and challenging situations you both have encountered and aided each other through?

____

____

____

____

4. **The Balancing Act:** Balancing the intricacies of one's personal life and professional career can often prove to be quite a delicate task. However, by cultivating a deeper understanding and fostering a supportive environment, this seemingly formidable challenge can be overcome, enabling us to lead more harmonious and well-rounded lives. Reflecting upon a time in which this delicate equilibrium was disrupted, describe the measures you both undertook to restore balance and reclaim a more harmonious existence? ____

____

____

____

5. **The Growth:** Reflecting on the profound evolution of your professional journey throughout the years and acknowledging the indispensable role that both of you have played in nurturing this growth, how have each of you consistently supported and uplifted one another as you advance in your careers?

____

____

____

____

Reflect and Connect

Here are some prompts to help you reflect on your career journey:

1. **Our Careers:** Discuss your career goals. How do they align with your personal life and relationship? ____

____

____

____

2. **Our Support:** Share instances where you felt supported by your partner in your career. How did it impact your professional and personal life?_

____

____

____

____

3. **Our Challenges:** Discuss the challenges you've faced in balancing your career and personal life. How did you overcome them?

____

____

____

____

4. **Our Future:** What are your future career aspirations? How can you support each other to achieve them? ____

____

____

____

Remember, attaining a flourishing career need not require sacrificing a prosperous relationship, and vice versa. Through the cultivation of mutual respect, comprehension, and backing, you and your partner can deftly navigate your respective career pathways while simultaneously fortifying the bond that binds you. May this chapter serve as a catalyst for introspection, aiding you in your quest to chart a fulfilling trajectory in your professional endeavors.

> " Success becomes exponentially more blissful when it is shared
> with the one who holds your heart."
> – Mike & Carol Byrd

Chapter Eight – Health and Wellness Choices

Embracing a healthier lifestyle together

A Healthy and Vibrant Life: This chapter revolves around one of the most pivotal aspects of your existence - health and wellness. It encapsulates the act of making intentional decisions for a flourishing lifestyle, upholding, and encouraging one another in these choices, and treasuring the dynamism and effervescence it bestows upon your lives.

- Values: Define your health and wellness values.

  ____
- ____
- ____

- Goals: Set wellness goals for yourselves and as a couple.

  ____
- ____
- ____
- ____

- Steps: Develop a plan for maintaining physical and mental well-being.

  ____
- ____
- ____
- ____
- ____

Landmark Moments

1.The Health Goals: Setting health and wellness goals together signifies the initiation of a transformative journey towards a healthier lifestyle. What or who were the catalysts for this change?

----

2. The Workout Buddy: Engaging in physical activities as a couple not only enhances your physical well-being but also nurtures your relationship, creating an enjoyable and fulfilling experience. What types of invigorating exercises have you both shared?

----

3. The Healthy Habits: Integrating wholesome habits into your daily routine, whether it's maintaining a well-balanced diet, engaging in regular exercise, or ensuring adequate rest. What are the healthy practices that both of you have brought into the relationship and still uphold?

----

4. The Challenges: Conquering health obstacles or setbacks together ultimately fortifies the bond you share. What struggles have you both encountered,
    and triumphed over?

----

5. The Vibrant Life: Reveling in the multitude of benefits that a healthy lifestyle bestows - the boundless energy, the infectious positivity, and the profound happiness it cultivates. How have you observed the advantageous impact of adopting a healthy way of life on your relationship?

Reflect and Connect

Here are some prompts to help you reflect on your health and wellness journey:

1. **Our Health Goals:** Discuss your shared health and wellness goals. How are you supporting each other in achieving them?

----

2. **Our Healthy Habits:** Share your daily health and wellness routine. How has it improved your life and relationship?

----

3. **Our Challenges:** Discuss any health challenges you've faced and how you overcame them together. ____

----

4. Our Future: What are your future health and wellness aspirations? How can you support each other to achieve them? ____

____

____

____

Remember, good health is a true treasure, and adopting a healthy lifestyle is an invaluable gift that both you and your loved ones can cherish. Let us nourish this gift, nurture it, and relish the vibrant and fulfilling life it bestows upon us. I sincerely hope that this chapter serves as a gentle reminder for you to ponder upon your journey towards optimal health and wellness.

> "Health is the foundation to create the life of your dreams.
> – Mike & Carol Byrd

Chapter Nine – Becoming Empty Nesters

Rediscovering Each Other

This chapter explores a fresh chapter in your journey together, when your children have matured and flown the nest, leaving you both with an abode that echoes with emptiness. It's a period of introspection, rediscovery, and a newfound bond that transcends the boundaries of conventional togetherness.

- Values: Identify the values that will guide your empty nest phase.

  ____

- ____

- ____

- ____

- Goals: What do you want to achieve as a couple now that the kids have left home?

  ____

- ____

- ____

- ____

- Steps: Discuss how you'll navigate this transition and reconnect with each other____

- ____

- ____

- ____

Landmark Moments

1. The Last Goodbye: As your child sets off on their own journey, bidding farewell becomes an emotional turning point, heralding the dawn of a new chapter in your life. Describe the profound depths of your emotions in that moment.

----

2. The Silence: Returning to a tranquil abode, now devoid of the familiar echoes of laughter, lively conversations, and occasional chaos, presents an uncanny experience. Delve into the realm of this newfound stillness and reflect on how both of you navigated through it.

----

3. Rediscovery: Blessed with an abundance of time dedicated solely to each other, you embark on a journey of rediscovery—a path filled with delightful encounters with your partner, your personal passions reignited, and even revelations about your own self. Unfold the treasured revelations and discoveries that have graced your lives.

----

4. New Routines: Embracing the beauty of change, you both craft a tapestry of new routines, weaving together experiences that revolve solely around the two of you. Shed light on the vibrant tapestry you have begun to create, showcasing the cherished moments that have become integral to your shared lives.

----

5. The Joy of Reunion: Erupting with unadulterated bliss, your children's return to the heart of your home filling the air with resounding laughter and enchanting stories. Share the memory of the first magnificent event that breathed life into your home once more, evoking overwhelming joy in both of your hearts.

Reflect and Connect

Here are some prompts to help you reflect on your journey as empty nesters:

1. **Our Emotions:** Discuss the feelings you experienced when you first became empty nesters. How have these feelings evolved over time between you both?

Spouse #1

Spouse #2

----

2. **Rediscovery:** How have you rediscovered each other in this new phase of life?

----

3. New Routines: Share your new routines and experiences. How have they brought you closer?

----

4. Looking Forward: What are you looking forward to in this new phase of your life?

Remember, the empty nest does not merely symbolize the conclusion of a journey, but rather the inception of a fresh one. It presents a unique opportunity to reconnect with one another and embrace life together through an entirely new lens. May this gentle reminder serve as an inspiration to both you and your partner as you navigate this uncharted phase of existence.

> An empty nest presents itself as an exquisite gateway for the expansion and deepening of the heart, inviting a fuller flourishing of love and connection.
> - Mike & Carol Byrd

Chapter Ten – Caring for Elderly Parents

Supporting Aging Loved Ones

In this poignant chapter, we delve into a profound stage of existence where the dynamics of caretaking take an unexpected turn, requiring us to assume the role of caregiver for our aging parents. It is a remarkable period of reciprocity, marked by the profound act of giving back, expressing heartfelt gratitude, and savoring precious moments shared with them.

- Values: Define the values that will underpin your caregiving role.
  - ____
  - ____
  - ____
  - ____
- Goals: What responsibilities and goals do you have as caregivers?
  - ____
  - ____
  - ____
- Steps: Plan how you'll provide physical and emotional support to your elderly parents.
  - ____
  - ____
  - ____
  - ____

Landmark Moments

1. The Realization: The moment when the realization dawns upon you that your parents are advancing in years and may require your support is indeed a profound and contemplative experience. It is a juncture that is brimming with a myriad of emotions, evoking an amalgamation of sentiments. As you reflect on this epiphany, what thoughts and reflections arose within you both?

Spouse #1

Spouse #2

----

2. The Role Reversal: The transition into the role of a caregiver can unquestionably be perplexing, perhaps even arduous at times. Yet, it is a responsibility that bestows upon you an opportunity for immense personal growth and fulfillment. Could you recount the instance when you encountered the most formidable circumstances in this new role?

----

3. The Bonding: Tending to the needs of your parents has the potential to forge deeply cherished bonds and give rise to moments of profound connection. These fleeting instants become ingrained in our hearts as lasting memories. Can you vividly describe the most extraordinary moment of such a bond that you experienced?

4. The Challenges: This path you have chosen is not devoid of hurdles, for both you as a couple and your parents. Physical, emotional, and logistical tests may assail your journey. Yet, in the face of these trials, it is crucial to remember that you are not traversing this path alone. How did you find solace together and overcome the most arduous challenge hand in hand with your parents?

____

____

____

____

5. The Gratitude: Expressing profound gratitude for the immeasurable contributions your parents have made to your life leaves an unforgettable mark, creating heartwarming memories that shall endure throughout your lifetime. What aspect of your parents' impact are you most profoundly grateful for?

____

____

____

____

Reflect and Connect

Here are some prompts to help you reflect on your journey of caring for your elderly parents:

1. Our Feelings: Share your feelings when you first realized your parents, or your partners parents needed your care. How have these feelings evolved over time?

Spouse #1

____

____

Spouse #2

____

____

2. Memorable Moments: Discuss any special moments or memories you have had while caring for your parents.

____

____

____

____

____

3. Our Challenges: What challenges have you faced as a couple in this journey and how have you overcome them together?

Spouse#1____

Spouse#2____

_+

4. Gratitude: Write a note of gratitude to your parents, acknowledging their contribution to your life. How does that make you feel?

____

____

____

____

Remember, this journey is about love, respect, and understanding. It's about giving back and saying 'thank you' in the most profound way possible. --- We hope this helps you explore and appreciate this phase of your journey together.

Compassion is the pivotal element that unlocks the depths of our capacity to provide tender and devoted care to our revered elders.

– Mike & Carol Byrd

Chapter Eleven Nurturing Shared Interests

Bonding Through Shared Passions

This chapter delves into the wondrous journey of uncovering and cultivating common passions. It encapsulates the sheer delight of engaging in activities together, embodying the essence of learning from one another, and forging cherished memories that invigorate the very fabric of your connection.

Landmark Moments

1. **The Discovery:** The moment you stumbled upon a mutual passion, a shared delight that transcended the ordinary. It could have been the sizzling symphony of flavors in the kitchen, the thrill of conquering nature's expanse through hiking, the captivating worlds unveiled in the pages of books, or the enchantment found in observing the graceful dance of birds in the wilderness. What unexpected treasure did you discover that rekindled delightful sparks of connection between you both?

   ----

2. The First Experience: In that blissful juncture where novelty intertwines with exhilaration, you embarked upon your voyage into the realm of your newfound passion. Your hearts united in anticipation, throbbing with excitement and the promise of boundless learning and unforgettable pleasure. Guided by the invisible hand of curiosity, you embarked on a joint expedition, your spirits soaring as they reveled in the sheer joy of discovery. What was the pinnacle of that journey, the cherished memory of your first venture together?

----

3. The Regular Activity: Together, you have woven your shared passion into the tapestry of your daily lives, creating a vibrant routine crafted from mutual devotion and laughter. You have fashioned a sanctuary of shared experiences, stitching threads of memory into the very fabric of your being. Every stroke of the clock brought you closer, as you have painted your lives with hues of enchantment and created an endless collage of treasured moments. How have you both embraced theses shared experiences?

Spouse #1

Spouse #2

----

4. The Challenges: As you delved deeper into your chosen pursuits, you may have encountered obstacles that tested you both, challenges that beckoned you to rise above the situations. It might have been a culinary experience that demanded mastering a complex recipe, or a demanding DIY endeavor that required your combined ingenuity. Regardless of the endeavor, your unbeatable spirits and shared determination propelled you through the storm, emerging stronger and more resolute. What has been the challenge that forged your bond, and shared triumph in the face of overwhelming odds?

----

5. The Joy: Amidst this exquisite symphony of shared delight, you discovered a harmonious melody that resonated within your very souls. Together, you reveled in the intoxicating euphoria of shared passions, your hearts entwined in a dance of pure joy. What magnificent treasure have you both uncovered, a shared joy that binds your hearts?

Reflect and Connect

Here are some prompts to help you reflect on your shared interests:

1. **Our Interests:** Discuss your shared interests. How did you discover them and what do you love about them?____

2. **Our Experiences:** Share your favorite experience related to your shared interests. What made it special? ____

____

____

____

3. **Our Challenges:** Discuss any challenges you've faced and how you overcame them together.

____

____

____

____

4. Our Future: Are there any new interests you would like to explore together in the future?

Remember, shared interests are not just about the activity itself; it's about the quality time spent together, the shared experiences, and the deeper connection it fosters. --- We hope this chapter helps you reflect on your shared interests and the joy they bring to your lives

Chapter Twelve – Envisioning the Future

Landmark Moments

1. The Dream: The first time you shared your aspirations and envisioned a future together, filled with hopes and dreams. This moment holds great significance, as it allows you to align your life paths and embrace a collective vision. What are the dreams you both hold dear, as a couple?

----

2. The Plan: Embarking on the exhilarating journey of turning your dreams into reality; a process that involves crafting a comprehensive plan encompassing goals, timelines, and strategic approaches. Together, you shape a roadmap towards making your shared dreams come true. What are the plans that you both envision?

----

3. The Steps: Initiating your grand plan, taking those crucial initial steps towards the realization of your dreams. Whether it calls for diligently saving funds for your dream abode, contemplating the beautiful prospect of starting a family, or meticulously preparing for that blissful stage of retirement, take the time to identify the first step of your plan and chart a well-defined timeline. What is your agreed upon timeline?

----

4. The Adjustments: Embracing life's unpredictable nature, where change and unforeseen circumstances often arise. This crucial phase demands resilience and adaptability, as you navigate the need to adjust your plans accordingly. Together, you face these challenges head-on, forging strength from your unyielding bond. What adjustments have you both gracefully made, knowing that flexibility is integral to the journey?

Spouse #1

____

____

Spouse #2

____

____

5. The Progress: A moment of serene reflection, a pause to marvel at how far you've come on the path towards realizing your shared dreams. Take the opportunity to appreciate the milestones achieved, while also acknowledging that exciting and fulfilling endeavors still lie ahead. How close or far are you both from accomplishing those future dreams that dance within your hearts?

Spouse #1

____

Spouse #2

____

Reflect and Connect

Here are some prompts to help you reflect on your journey towards the future:

1. Our Dreams: Discuss your shared dreams for the future. How have they evolved over time?

____

____

2. Our Plan: Share your plan for realizing these dreams. How have you supported each other in this process?

____

____

____

____

3. Our Steps: Reflect on the steps you've taken towards your future. What were the challenges and victories?

____

____

____

____

____

____

4. Our Future: What does your envisioned future look like now? How can you work together to realize it? ____

____

____

____

____

Remember, the future is not set in stone. It's a canvas on which you paint your dreams, one brushstroke at a time. With love, support, and shared dreams, you can create a beautiful future together. --- we hope these chapters have helped you reflect on your journey and strengthened your bond.

Bonus Chapter- Our Rules for Engagement

Nurturing Healthy Communication and Conflict Resolution

In any interpersonal connection, the key pillars of success lie in the art of effective communication and conflict resolution. This enlightening chapter shall serve as your guiding light towards constructing a comprehensive framework of principles and agreements that will gracefully steer you through the treacherous waters of disagreements, misinterpretations, and challenging conversations, all while upholding the sacred values of love and respect.

Values: Identifying Shared Communication Values

- Take some time to discuss and write down the values you both hold dear when it comes to communication. These values will serve as the foundation for your rules of engagement.

Spouse #1 ____
____
Spouse #2 ____
____

Step 1: Active Listening

- Agree to actively listen to each other without interrupting.
- Use non-verbal cues to show you're engaged, such as nodding and maintaining eye contact.
- Summarize what you've heard to ensure understanding before responding.

Step 2: Expressing Emotions

- Encourage open expression of emotions without judgment or criticism.
- Use "I" statements to express feelings and thoughts, i.e., "I feel hurt when..."
- Avoid blaming language and name-calling.

Step 3: Time-Outs

- Recognize the need for breaks during heated discussions.
- Establish a "time-out" signal or word that either partner can use to pause the conversation.
- Commit to returning to the conversation when emotions have cooled.

Step 4: Fair Fighting

- Agree on rules for fair fighting, such as no yelling, name-calling, or bringing up past issues.
- Focus on the issue at hand and avoid using unrelated grievances as ammunition.

Step 5: Resolution and Compromise

- Commit to finding solutions and compromises together.
- Understand that it's okay to agree to disagree on some matters.
- Seek win-win solutions that benefit both partners.

Step 6: Forgiveness and Letting Go

- Embrace forgiveness as a crucial part of conflict resolution.
- Agree not to hold grudges or bring up resolved issues in future disagreements.
- Remember that forgiving doesn't mean forgetting but moving forward with love.

Step 7: Privacy and Discretion

- Respect each other's privacy and discretion when discussing personal matters.
- Avoid sharing intimate details or airing grievances with others without consent.
- Understand the importance of maintaining trust within your relationship.

Step 8: Seek Support When Needed

- Recognize that sometimes you may need outside help.
- Be open to seeking couples counseling or guidance when communication becomes challenging.

- Set a schedule for revisiting and updating your rules of engagement.
- Ensure that they continue to reflect your evolving needs and values as a couple.

> "Effective communication is the bridge that connects hearts,
> and builds understanding."
> – Mike & Carol Byrd

Your rules of engagement serve as the blueprint that nurtures and sustains a healthy, affectionate, and respectful relationship between the two of you. Embrace these invaluable principles as the ultimate tools to fortify the foundation of your connection, enabling you both to weather the storms of life together. Always bear in mind that disagreements, rather than disruptive obstacles, are transformative opportunities for personal growth and mutual understanding. By consistently honoring and valuing each other's beliefs, desires, and emotional needs, you'll not only foster a resilient partnership, but also continue to construct a profound and enduring bond.

Conclusion:

Congratulations on taking the steps in pinning your vision together in completing "Our Life Together." May this visionary journal serve as a steadfast compass to navigate your partnership through life's myriad seasons. Bear in mind that love, open communication, and mutually shared aspirations are the fundamental pillars of an enduring and gratifying relationship. Embrace the enthralling voyage together and beget a treasure trove of everlasting, enchanting memories.

About The Authors

Meet Mike and Carol Byrd, the celebrated authors of "Our Life Together," a heartwarming couples' journal that invites you to embark on a journey of shared memories, emotions, and dreams. With their extensive experience as relationship coaches, Mike and Carol bring a unique perspective to the art of preserving your love story.

About Mike and Carol Byrd:

Mike and Carol have spent over two decades guiding couples towards deeper, more meaningful relationships. Their expertise in nurturing love and emotional intimacy has touched the lives of countless individuals and couples worldwide. They are passionate about helping couples connect on a profound level, and this journal is a testament to their commitment.

Why "Our Life Together" Is Special:

- **Guided Storytelling:** Mike and Carol Byrd provide insightful prompts to inspire your reflections, feelings, and aspirations for a more enduring connection.
- **Celebrating Love:** This journal is a heartfelt celebration of your love story. It's a space to capture your unique moments and memories.
- **Strengthening Bonds:** Sharing your experiences and dreams in this journal deepens the emotional connection between you and your partner.
- **A Legacy of Love:** "Our Life Together" becomes a cherished keepsake, preserving your love story for future generations.

Mike and Carol Byrd's "Our Life Together" is more than just a journal; it's a testament to the power of love and the art of storytelling. It's your canvas to paint the picture of your unique journey together. Start documenting your love story today.

All graphics were created in Canva with AI